MW01644755

Speak to me little one,
Clutching my breast with your hand,
So strong and firm for all its littleness.
It will be the hand of a warrior, my son,
A hand that will gladden your father.
See how eagerly it fastens on me:
It thinks already of a spear.
O son, you will have a warrior's name and
be a leader of men.

African proverb

The Book of African Names

As told by

CHIEF <u>O</u>SUNTOKI

BLACK CLASSIC PRESS
P.O. BOX 13414
BALTIMORE, MD 21203
A Young Press With Some Very Old Ideas

The Book of African Names

PUBLISHED 1991 BY
BLACK CLASSIC PRESS

Our thanks to the former coordinators of Drum and Spear Press for permission to republish this book.

Cover design by Julee Thompson

Library of Congress Card Catalog Number 90- 082690
ISBN:0- 933121- 24- 5

Founded in 1978 Black Classic Press specializes in bringing to light obscure and significant works by and about people of African descent. If our books are not available in your area ask your local bookseller to order them. Our current list of titles can be obtained by writing:

BLACK CLASSIC PRESS
c/o List
P.O. Box 13414
Baltimore, MD 21203
A Young Press With Some Very Old Ideas

Among Africans, children are the carriers of the future.

Placed upon the children is the whole sacred trust of African heritage. The Race itself finds endless longevity in them. Our children carry from us and our ancestors a total spiritual and human endowment and extend our sacred heritage to their offspring and to African generations yet to come. Children are the buds of society, and every birth is the arrival of spring, when life shoots out and the community thrives. The birth of an African child then can not only be the concern and the joy of the parents but of many relatives and members of the community at large now living and also long departed.

The child is brought into the world by an act of union and creation by the blood parents but it is the whole community that develops the child into a social being and into a person full of the African personality. It is the Naming of the child that first begins the establishment of the child's personal identity. It is the Naming of the child also that first brings upon the child some general recognition by the community at large. For these reasons the Naming of the child among Africans is an occasion of some importance and, no matter how modestly performed, the act of Naming the child is attended with some ceremony. Of course among the great African communities today the Naming ceremony cannot be uniform in its performance. Nowadays we live too scattered apart. The young, as you already know, have fallen away from the strict practices of the elders. The young also have adopted for their own positive use many of the creative ideas of this age upon us now. But our people, for one great era of silence, lived in terrible bondage. It was then that we were forced to take on foreign names and to be weakened in the defense of our heritage. And it is true as we can see so clearly that in great numbers we were taken to foreign lands. To survive, we took on the speaking of foreign tongues. And, in time, you know, we began to forget how the African gets his name. It is strange, indeed, it hurts my heart, that brothers from afar often come to greet me bearing such names as "Willie", "Juan" and "François". But we can not be hard against them, for they have been misled. My own attendant, Ladipo̱, tells me that in the lands afar many Africans there are throwing off these names but that they still do not know how to come by their proper birthright.

So I, Osuntoki, will tell them of their birthright and how they may seek their names. And the lessons I give to you now, let them be written so that all may see.

THE NAMING-DAY CEREMONY

The Naming-Day Ceremony

The Naming-Day ceremony is held seven to ten days following the birth of the African child. This is true for both boy and girl children. For in our community, every new child is fully welcome and no distinctions of inequality exist at birth.

Nowadays it is common practice, especially in African communities of the West, for mothers to be attended at childbirth in hospitals. Parents are asked to state the name of their child for identification and registration purposes. At this time, parents of the community should merely indicate that their surname be placed on the identification bracelet of their newborn child.

The birth certificate should be filled out and recorded after the Naming-Day ceremony takes place. Appropriate invitations to family and friends can be issued immediately following the safe delivery of the child.

The Naming-Day ceremony is held at the home of the parents, either mid-morning or early afternoon. Grandparents, aunts, uncles, cousins, in-laws and other members of the community are present to celebrate the arrival of a new member in their midst. As they enter the house, each person leaves at the door some small token of good-will, some item of clothing or wrap for the child; something that will be especially useful to the parents or given the coming of the child something for the household itself. Relatives and friends, if they are female, give their gifts to the child's mother, and the men present their gifts to the child's father. An elder woman holds the child. After water is sprinkled towards the ceiling, the elder woman stroking the child's head whispers the name into the child's ear to implant the name in the baby's head. The significance of this act is to separate the child from the spirit world where he is only an object, thus marking the child's entry into the community of human beings.

When the name has been given the child has been introduced to life itself.

The remainder of the time is spent festively. Relatives and friends enjoy the company of each other. And at the same time they collectively seal their sense of communion with the child. Of course a feast of food is prepared and brought by some of the guests themselves. People attending the Naming-Day ceremony sit about talking to each other making well wishes in the name of the child. Or, as is always the case when such kinsmen gather, talk extends to things both near and far as they affect daily life. Some people, the young (as well as the elders) dance too. All of this goes on for more than several hours. And to keep the event lively preparations begin probably two days beforehand. Once the Naming-Day ceremony is ending people simply file away making favored wishes upon the child, upon the parents and upon the household.

HOW KOFI GOT HIS NAME

How Kofi Got His Name

Now then, I have yet to explain how the name of the child is actually chosen. Often among our people, the name chosen for the child marks the occasion of his birth. For example, if the child comes during a time of planting crops, he would be given a name meaning 'planting' or 'growing'. Another way the name might be chosen is to consider the state of the house or other circumstances connected with the child and his family. For instance, among the Yoruba-speakers:

Ayodele	***means***	***Joy enters the house***
Onipe̱de	***means***	***The consoler is come***
Iyapo̱	***means***	***Many trials***

Sometimes it is the practice among the Yoruba to choose for a child a name that shows a deity worshipped by the family. Take for example those who worship Shango, Yoruba god of thunder and lightning; a child's name can be:

Shangobunmi	***which means***	***child given by Shango***

OR

Ogunṣẹyẹ	***which means***	***Ogun, the Yoruba god of war, has done the becoming thing.***

Among our people the child will pick up other names as he grows up. This can go on endlessly. But usually one name of endearment sticks with the child. The pet name or 'nickname' usually expresses what a child is or what the child is hoped to become. To males we attribute names of strength, bravery and

heroic deeds. Let me give you more examples from the Yorubas.

Males

Ajamu	one who seizes after a fight
Ajagbe	one who carries off after a contest
Akinlawon Okanlawon	one who comes after a family has had several female children

Females

Ayoka	one who brings joy to all
Asabi	one of select birth
Alake	one to be petted and looked after

It is told to me by Ladipo and I know it to be correct that among our brothers in the East, the speakers of Luo, the name is sought for while the infant is crying. Different names of the ancestors are recited and, if the child stops crying when a particular name is called, the child receives that name as a mark of favor.

Sometimes among the Kikuyu, more of our brothers on the East African shores, a first-born son is simply given a name in honor of his father. Mwangi Kago is named so because he is Mwangi-son-of-Kago. Kago the father is Kago-son-of-Mwangi, Mwangi being his father; thus, the generations are always linked through the first-born son. Mwangi Kago will of course name his first son Kago-son-of Mwangi.

I, Osuntoki, once had a chance to be on a journey for more than two months. I travelled far. I travelled to the West where our brothers speak in the Akan tongues. There among the Akan I talked with one more ancient than I and having all manner of *wisdom. Now I do not know if he lives or if he departs. But in our talks he told me, O̲suntoki, that the children among the Akan receive their names from their fathers or the head of the father's family. And that among them children bear a first name, Akeradini (the soul's name), according to the day of the week on which they are born. The first name is declared and pronounced by the person who attends the mother at the time of the delivery. These Ghanaians do not believe that anybody gives the child this first part of his name. "He is born with it; he comes with it," they say. So for the Akeradini there is no ceremony because the child has this name at the very hour of birth.*

The second main part of a Ghanaian name is said to

be Agyadini (the father's name). So responsibility falls upon the father to bestow to the child this part of his name.

The Agyadini does take place at the high point of a ceremony, Adinto (naming), Mpuei (outdooring), when relatives and friends have gathered to show how fond they are of the one who is to bear the name. The Naming time comes early in the morning of the seventh day after the day on which the child is born. For this name the father has to look to the distinguished of his own father's house to find a name that fits the dignity of the child.

Day of Week		Birthday Names		Child of:
English	Akan	Male	Female	Akan Meaning
Saturday	Memenda	Kwame	Ama	Most ancient
Sunday	Kwasida	Kwesi	Akosua	Under the sun
Monday	Dwouda	Kwadwo	Adwoa	Peace
Tuesday	Benada	Kwabena	Abena	Fire
Wednesday	Wukuda	Kwaku	Akua	Fame
Thursday	Yaoda	Yao (Yaw)	Yaa	Strength
Friday	Frida	Kofi	Afua	Growth

Among another of our people in the west, the Igbo, the day of name-giving for a child is marked by a gathering of the total family group. Much food and drink is prepared for the ceremony. The Igbo feel that the total experience of the family as well as characteristics of the child are important in the giving of names. Presents of money and food are brought by all of the guests to show their goodwill towards the infant and to celebrate his or her acceptance into the society.

The child is displayed to his family and friends in a ceremony called an 'outing'. The baby may receive the name of the market-day on which he was born, NwaOkoerie, for instance, meaning a male child born on Orie market day. He may also be called Chukwuemeka meaning 'God has done well' which is a thanksgiving name. And he might too be called Onwubiko meaning 'May death forgive", relating to his parents' loss of other children and the hope for survival of this one. The whole ceremony lasts for one day.

Among our brothers in the East, the Nyamwezi, children receive their names within a few days of their birth. It is against tradition that they should be named after anyone in the same age-set as their own parents. A child of the Nyamwezi usually is named after a grandparent and is also given a name that tells what occurred or what event took place at the time of birth.

A boy born in the morning, for instance, is called Misana. Among our Nyamwezi brothers, boy and girl children may receive related names, Mabula (male), and Kabula (female), but mostly their names differ. Twins receive special names as do children who come feet first from their mothers.

The Naming ceremony is carried out five days following birth when the infant is brought forth from the childbirth hut and shown to family and clan members gathered for the great occasion.

Now we must understand that the ways of keeping faith with the Creator are different within many African communities. In the far North, I am told, where our brothers, the Hausa, live, they follow the ways of Islam and pray to Allah.

Our Hausa brothers perform the Naming ceremony seven days after a child is born. The father of the child's father slaughters a ram and his wife gives new cloth to the child's mother. Before the actual giving of the name, the baby is carried off by the mid-wife to have his head shaven clean.

For the male child, his name is witnessed only by the religious scribes, the Malams, and other males of his family. They come and stand at the entrance of the childbirth hut to give the child his name. Next the kinsmen give away three gourds of kola nuts, if the child is a boy, and two for a girl child. The baby is returned to his mother who refuses to hold him. Only after much urging by her kinswomen will she suckle the child and only away from curious eyes.

During the Hausa ceremony there is drumming throughout the day and all night. The whole community gives money away on behalf of its newest member.

Not too far away in other parts of our lands, Sierra Leone, Guinea, Senegal, the faithful of Islam observe the Naming ceremony in ways akin to the Hausa one.

When such an event is to occur all of the neighboring chiefs, councillors and elders are called forth to attend. The women of the compound prepare much food for that day. When the elder men arrive they are warmly greeted by the chief of the area where the ceremony is taking place.

Next the guests present their gifts of kola nuts, fruits, livestock and gold jewelry. A special cow is brought into the gathering and tethered.

The religious men, Imams, also preside as the drums begin to announce the event. The mother, wearing beautiful dress of head-tie, overblouse and richly-printed lapa cloth, comes out of her house with the baby and sits on a low stool. She also wears gold earrings, necklace, bracelets and rings. An elder comes forward and shaves the child's head. Then the chief Imam steps up and formally asks the name of the child. The ceremony goes like this:

Chief Imam: What is to be the name of this child?

Chief Elder: His name is (Amu).

The Imam turns to all assembled and in a loud voice calls the name. Amu! Amu! Amu!

At this call, one of the men takes his knife and slashes the cow's throat. Then the chief Imam offers a prayer.

> *In the name of Allah, The Compassionate, The Merciful. We have named this child, Amu, today. May he zealously learn the faith of Allah as he grows up. Throughout his life, may nothing separate him from that faith. May he be charitable in all his doings, just and true towards his fellowmen. Amin.*

The mother next takes the baby into the house as more Imams offer prayers to the child's good fortune. Then the great drum is sounded to announce the end of the formal ceremony. The beef is distributed to all present who then drift away to return only at sunset.

At this time, drummers, singers, dancers and other musicians gather in front of the chief's house. The men play on harps and sing the chief's praises. Next the women join in the celebration and perform special dances to the ceremonial drums. The chief and his councillors watch the festivities and give away gold bars and cloth to the dancers.

A child receiving a Name is a sign of union with our ancestors and for us, who still wander upon the dry earth and the waters of the sea, it is a mark of identification and respect. The Name is the link with our father's past and the past of their fathers. Now that I, Ọsuntoki, have given you the true path of our ancestors let no man lead you off the road they walk.

Wo isọ de mi ko le jọ onisọ

SOME POPULAR AFRICAN NAMES

GIRLS NAMES FROM WEST AFRICA

Name	*Meaning*
Binta	***With God***
Nini	***Stone***
Okolo	***Friendly***
Bisa	***Greatly loved***
Soyini	***Richly endowed***
Tene	***Love***
Ashaki	***Beautiful***
Tiombe	***Shy***
Tuere	***Sacred***
Koumba	***Helper***
Abena	***Pure***
Amma	***Famous***
Adjua	***Noble***
Kai	***Lovable***
Serwaa	***Jewel***
Afi	***Spiritual***
Akua	***Sweet Messenger***
Nana	***Mother of the Earth***
Fatou Mata	***Beloved by all***
Assata	***Warlike***
Mayimuna	***Expressive***
Bintou	***Royal***
Djenaba	***Affectionate***
Assitou	***Careful***
Oure	***Saintly***
Abi	***to guard***
Aminata	***Good character***
Eintou	***Pearl***
Mariama	***Gift of God***
Malene	***Tower***
Fanta	***Beautiful day***
Nalo	***Much loved***
Saran	***Joy***
Sadio	***Pure***
Manana	***Lustrous***
Noni	***Gift of God***
Ahurole	***Loving***
Ayeola	***Rainbow***
Nini	***Industrious***
Ama	***Happy***
Efuru	***Daughter of Heaven***
Onyema	***Sorrow***
Nneka	***Tender***
Adama	***Majestic***
Nkechi	***Loyal***
Njeri	***Anointed***
Ngozi	***Blessing***
Hawanya	***A Tear***
Laraba	***Wednesday***
Marka	***steady rain***
Fitima	***Evening, dusk***

Yoruba

Name	*Meaning*	*Sex*
Ambe	***We begged God for it***	***M/F***
Aiyetoro	***Peace on earth***	***M/F***
Ayo	***Joy***	***F***
Ayodele	***Joy comes home***	***F***
Aduke	***much loved***	***F***
Adeleke	***the crown gets on top***	***F***
Abiola	***child born during first days of the New Year***	***M***
Akintunde	***a boy has come again***	***M***
Akinwunmi	***like a hero /warrior***	***M***
Akinlabi	***We have a boy***	***M***
Adelaja	***the crown settles the quarrel***	***M***
Bandele	***born away from home***	***M***
Babatunde	***Father comes again***	***F***
Bosede	***born on Sunday***	***F***
Olufemi	***God loves me***	***F***
Oluremi	***God consoles me***	***F***
Olufunke	***God gives me to love***	***F***
Olufunmilayo	***God gives me joy***	***F***

Yoruba

Name	*Meaning*	*Sex*
Olujimi	*God gave me this*	*M*
Olutosin	*God deserves to be praised*	*M*
Olatunde	*Joy comes again*	*M*
Owodunni	*It is nice to have money*	*M*
Omotunde	*a child comes again*	*M*
Oluremi	*God consoles*	*F*
Olabisi	*Joy is multiplied*	*F*
Foluke	*Placed in God's hands*	*M/F*
Jumoke	*Everyone loves the child*	*M/F*
Kayode	*He brought joy*	*M*
Olaniyi	*There's glory in wealth*	*F*
Modupe	*Thank you*	*M*
Temitope	*Thanks to God*	*F*
Yetunde	*Mother comes again*	*F*
Kehinde	*Twin who comes second*	*M*
Taiwo	*Twin who comes first*	*M*
Idowu	*born after twins*	*M*
Alaba	*born after Idowu*	*M*

Benin

Name	*Meaning*	*Sex*
Enobakhare	***what the Chief says***	***M***
Osayimwese	***God created me all right***	***M***
Obaseki	***the Oba surpasses the market***	***M***
Odion	***the first of twins***	***M***
Omwokha	***the second of twins***	***M***
Ode	***one born along the road***	***M/F***
Omolara	***child born at the right time***	***M/F***
Enomwoyi	***one who has grace, charm***	***F***
Oseye	***the happy one***	***F***
Osayande	***God owns the world***	***M***
Osayaba	***God forgives***	***M***
Osakwe	***God agrees***	***M***
Osahar	***God hears***	***M***
Osaze	***Whom God likes***	***M***

Akan

Name	*Meaning*	*Sex*
Abena	***Manly in bearing***	***M***
Ako	***the first child***	***M***
Ano	***the second child***	***M***
Asa or Anse	***the third child***	***M/F***
Anapa	***Morning***	***F***
Okera	***a likeness to God***	***M***
Edo	***Love***	***F***
Ahoto	***Peace***	***M***
Ede	***Sweetness***	***F***
Ahonya	***Prosperity***	***M***
Anika	***Goodness***	***F***
Antobam	***the sufferer***	***M***
Osei	***Maker of the great***	***M***
Owusu	***the clearer of the way***	***M***

BOYS NAMES FROM WEST AFRICA

Name	Meaning	Name	Meaning
Diallo	*Bold*	Atiim	*Violent*
Dia	*Champion*	Atiba	*Understanding*
Kandia	*Fortress*	Kasimu	*Keeper of the forest*
Diarra	*Gift*	Toola	*Workman*
Sekou	*Fighter*	Jaja	*God's gift*
Diaba	*Cliff dweller*	N'namdi	*Worthy*
Guila	*Dark stranger*	Kashka	*Friendly*
Damani	*Thoughtful*	Idowu	*Famous*
Yameogo	*Wealthy*	Ajene	*True*
Konata	*Man of high station*	Butu	*Weary*
Khari	*Kingly*	Nantambu	*Man of destiny*
Jawara	*Peace loving*	Kambon	*of the People*
Idrissa	*Immortal*	Chinyelu	*Invincible*
Baye	*Straightforward*	Kwesi	*Conquering strength*
Enaharo	*Like the sun*	Azikiwe	*Healthy*
Okpara	*Shelter*	Nldamak	*World ruler*
Afiba	*By the sea*	Duguma	*Spear*
Fati	*Robust*	Modeira	*Teacher*
Abayomi	*Friend*	Nabate	*Little*
Babatu	*Peace maker*	Keita	*Worshipper*
Asinia	*Stern*	Modibo	*Helper*
Mongo	*Famous*	Kala	*Tall*
Obafemi	*Tall*	Birago	*Red earth*
Kojo	*Unconquerable*	Babu	*Willing*

BOYS NAMES FROM WEST AFRICA

Names	*Meaning*
Chicha	***Beloved***
Fela	***Warlike***
Soyica	***Thin***
Kobie	***Warrior***
Oji	***Giftbearer***
Kodjo	***Humourous***
Oraefo	***Affectionate***
Moriba	***Curious***
Karamoko	***Studious***
Abayomi	***Ruler of people***
Koro	***Golden***
Bloke	***Proud chief***
Ifoma	***Lasting friend***
Camara	***Teacher***
Italo	***Full of valor***
Balewa	***Happiness***
Sule	***Adventurous***

GIRLS NAMES FROM CENTRAL AFRICA

Name	*Meaning*
Kafi	*Quiet*
Migozo	*Earnest*
Nakpangi	*Star*
Adero	*Life giver*
Kemba	*Faithful*
Ndunga	*Famous*
Andito	*Great One*
Nalungo	*Beautiful*
Nazapa	*of sacrifice*
Nataki	*of high birth*
Lumengo	*Flower*
Zola	*Productive*
Nsombi	*Abounding joy*
Nsenga	*womanly delight*
Ndunba	*Happy*
Nzinga	*Beautiful*
Kilolo	*Youthful*
Mawakana	*Yielding*
Niambi	*Melody*
Nkenge	*Brilliant*

BOYS NAMES FROM CENTRAL AFRICA

Name	Meaning
Opio	*Liberated*
Tacuma	*Alert*
Oronde	*Appointed*
Yerodin	*Studious*
Kibwe	*Blessed*
Diop	*Ruler*
Nzinga	*From the river*
Yero	*Warrior*
Mani	*From the mountain*
Yamro	*Courteous*
Mwata	*Sensible*
Sanga	*From the valley*
Lumumba	*Gifted*
Kalonji	*Man of victory*
Diallobe	*Heroic*
Kanyama	*Guard*
Changa	*strong as iron*
Nogomo	*Prosperous*

Name	Meaning
Mutope	*Protector*
Kakuyon	*Maker of weapons*
Changamire	*Like the sun*
Dombo	*from another village*
Dunduza	*man of adventure*
Mugabe	*Athlete*
Kitaka	*Good farmer*
Lasana	*Poet*
Sokoni	*From the sea*
Nyahuma	*Helper of men*
Jawanza	*Dependable*
Cazembe	*Wise man*
Sinawothi	*Fox*
Komunyaka	*Passionate*
Kalomo	*The Unexpected*
Mainza	*Rich*
Mwanza	*Wise protector*

Acoli

Name	*Meaning*	*Sex*
Okang	***first son***	***M***
Oboi	***second son***	***M***
Odai	***third son***	***M***
Apiyo and Acen	***names for twins***	***M***
Akelo	***a son born after twins***	***M***
Adong	***a daughter whose father has died before her birth***	***F***

GIRLS NAMES FROM EAST AFRICA

Name	*Meaning*
Ayanna	***Beautiful flower***
Damali	***Beautiful vision***
Sala	***Gentle***
Najuma	***Abounding in joy***
Ewunike	***Fragrant***
Lubangi	***born in water***
Andaiye	***daughter comes home***
Wambui	***Singer of songs***
Mijiza	***works with hands***
Muga	***Mother of all***
Njeri	***belonging to a warrior***
Ngina	***one who serves***

Bajita

Name	*Meaning*	*Sex*
Maijo	*herd of cattle*	*M*
Mganga	*Herbalist, practicer of Medicine*	*M*
Mugeta	*one born at night*	*M*
Magoti	*born during time of tax collection*	*M*
Mukama	*born during chief's taking of office*	*M*
Maragesi	*born at the time of a wedding*	*M*
Mabula	*born during rainy season*	*M*
Muganda	*meaning of a bundle of grass or any container ½ full of water*	*M*
Machumu	*Spears, Warrior, Blacksmith*	*M*

BOYS NAMES FROM EAST AFRICA

Name	*Meaning*
Kagale	*Trouble*
Kahero	*conceived at home*
Abeid	*Leader*
Bomani	*Warrior*
Karume	*Forest keeper*
Seitu	*Artist*
Bhoke	*Wanderer*
Erasto	*Man of peace*
Babu	*Man of medicine*
Yusufu	*Enchanter*
Mugo	*Wise man*
Mombera	*Man of adventure*
Oding	*Wood carver*
Kimani	*Sailor*
Kenyatta	*Musician*
Muriu	*Unknown*
Jojo	*Story-teller*
Kiambu	*rich*
Kamau	*Quiet Warrior*

Name	*Meaning*
Njonjo	*Holy man*
Cacanja	*Medicine man*
Kambui	*Fearless*
Macharia	*Lasting friend*
Mwangi	*Father of many children*
Dedan	*Town dweller*
Mwando	*Good worker*
Segundo	*Large bird*
Jaramogi	*Traveller*
Oginga	*Drummer*
Mbiyu	*Fast runner*
Karanja	*Guide*
Alimayu	*in honor of God*
Ketema	*From the valley*
Zawdie	*Chosen leader*
Ato	*Brilliant*
Makonnen	*Ruler*

Ma-Shona

Name	*Meaning*	*Sex*
Mudiwa	*the loved*	*F*
Muchaneta	*You will get tired*	*F*
Chuma	*Wealth, beads*	*F*
Runako	*Beauty*	*F*
Chenzira	*Born on the road*	*F*
Rufaro	*Happiness*	*F*
Goredema	*Black cloud*	*M*
Sekayi	*to laugh*	*F*
Mashama	*You are surprised*	*F*
Spiwe	*We were given*	*F*
Maideyi	*What did you want?*	*F*
Chioneso	*Guiding light*	*F*
Pepukayi	*Wake up!*	*M/F*
Sondai	*to push*	*M*
Betserai	*to help*	*M*
Gamba	*Warrior*	*M*
Hondo	*War*	*M*
Tichawona	*We shall see*	*M*
Kokayi	*Summon the people*	*M*
Banga	*knife*	*M*
Rudo	*Love*	*F*
Chipo	*Gift*	*F*

BOYS NAMES FROM SOUTH AFRICA

Name	*Meaning*
Gaika	***Wood carver***
Momar	***Philosopher***
Matsimela	***the roots***
Muata	***Searcher***
Nkosi	***Ruler***
Sigidi	***a thousand***
Ayize	***Let it come***
Dingane	***a person in need***
Bayete	***between God and man***

NAMING RECORD

Head of Household

Mother

Name of Child

Date of Birth

Day of Birth

Date of Naming Ceremony

Origin of Name

Meaning of Name

Significance of Name

Celestial Guide

Sun Sign

Moon Sign

Birth Mark

Symbolic Stone